SOMETHING IN THE KITCHEN

Roger Stevens

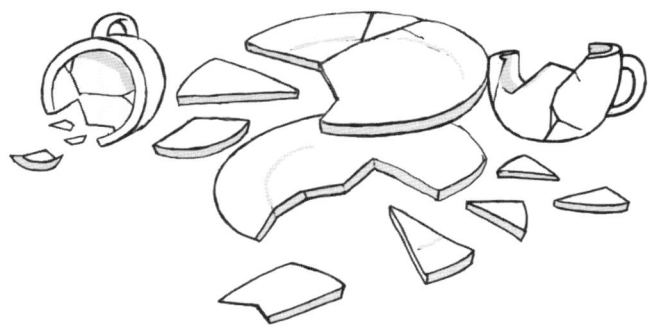

Illustrated by Graham Smith

Titles in First Flight

Phantom Striker
Pest Control
Shark's Fin Island
Scary!
Ping Pong with King Kong
The Fame Game
Awesome Animals
Big, Fast Rides

Car Boot Genie
Monster Cards
Ssh! My Family are Spies
Ghost Dog Mystery
Chip Boy
Sky Bikers
Surfing Three-Sixty
Something in the Kitchen
The Ghost in the Art Room
Robert and the Werewolf
The Biggest Lies Ever
Mad about Money

Badger Publishing Limited
15 Wedgwood Gate, Pin Green Industrial Estate,
Stevenage, Hertfordshire SG1 4SU
Telephone: 01438 356907. Fax: 01438 747015
www.badger-publishing.co.uk
enquiries@badger-publishing.co.uk

Something in the Kitchen ISBN 1 84424 842 9

Text © Roger Stevens 2006
Complete work © Badger Publishing Limited 2006

All rights reserved. No part of this publication may be reproduced, stored in any form or by any means mechanical, electronic, recording or otherwise without the prior permission of the publisher.

The right of Roger Stevens to be identified as author of this Work has been asserted by him in accordance with the Copyright, Designs and Patents Act 1988.

Series Editor: Jonny Zucker
Publisher: David Jamieson
Commissioning Editor: Carrie Lewis
Editor: Paul Martin
Design: Fiona Grant
Illustration: Graham Smith

SOMETHING IN THE KITCHEN
Roger Stevens

Contents

Don't fight 4
A ghost in the house 9
Locked out 12
A smashing time 19
A real-life ghost 26
Mad Mum 30

Don't fight

"I'm going to the shop," Mum said. "I won't be long. And don't fight while I'm gone."

"We won't," Jamie said. "We never fight, do we Sally?"

"No, we never fight," Sally said.

"Good. Now, you're in charge, Jamie. So look after your little sister."

"I will, Mum," Jamie said. "Can I have a Lucky Bag?"

"If you behave."

"And can I have a Curly Wurly?" Sally asked.

"She'll stick it up her nose," Jamie said.

"I won't."

"You did last time."

"Stop it!" Mum said. "Sally was only three when she did that."

Mum took her coat from the peg in the hall and opened the front door. A blast of cold rain blew in. "Remember – no fighting!"

"Okay. Bye, Mum," they both said.

The front door closed with a bang.

"I'm going to watch 'The Haunted House'," Jamie said.

Sally followed him into the front room. He turned on the TV and put on the DVD.

"Mum said I mustn't watch ghost stories," Sally said. "They give me bad dreams."

"Hard luck."

"I want to watch a cartoon."

"Well, you can't."

Sally grabbed the remote control and sat on it. The TV went dead.

"Give me that," Jamie yelled.

"No. I want to watch a cartoon."

"Give me that or the ghost will get you."

"No it won't," Sally said. "Don't be silly."

"Yes it will. Listen. It's coming."

"No it's not," Sally cried.

"The ghost is coming. Wooooooooo wooooooo. The ghost is coming after YOU!"

"Stop it!" Sally cried. She ran behind the armchair to hide.

"The ghost is coming. Here it comes. Wooooooooooo!"

Jamie grabbed the remote control and laughed.

A ghost in the house

BANG!

"What was that?" Jamie said.

"It's the ghost," Sally said.
She started to cry.

BANG!

There it was again.

"It's coming from the kitchen," Jamie said.

"It's the ghost!" Sally said.

"Don't be silly," Jamie said. "There are no such things as ghosts."
But Jamie wasn't so sure any more.

BANG!

"There's a ghost in the kitchen," Sally said.

"Maybe we'd better go outside,"
Jamie said, and went into the hall.

"Wait for me!"

Jamie opened the front door and went out into the rain.

Jamie thought, "I'm just being silly. Of course there are no ghosts." Suddenly there was a gust of wind and the door slammed shut.

Locked out

Jamie was locked out. He shouted through the letter box, "Let me in, I'm getting wet."

"I can't."

"Why not?"

"The lock is too stiff. I can't turn it."

BANG!

"It's the ghost!" Sally shouted.

"Wait there," Jamie said.

BANG!

The banging was coming from the side of the house. Jamie crept along the front of the house. Then he looked round the corner.

BANG!

The back gate was banging in the wind. Jamie went back to the front door to tell Sally.

"It's only the back gate banging in the wind," he told Sally.

"It's the ghost," Sally said.

"No it's not. There is no ghost. It's just the back gate. I'm coming in the kitchen door. Go and open it."

BANG!

"It's the ghost, it's the ghost!"

"SHUT UP!" Jamie shouted. "It's not a ghost. It's the back gate. Now go and open the kitchen door. I'm getting wet out here!"

Jamie ran round the house to the back yard. He shut the gate behind him.

As Jamie expected, the back door that led into the kitchen was locked.
Mum always kept it locked.

"Are you there?" Jamie called to Sally.

"Yes."

He could just about hear Sally's voice over the wind and rain.

"Open the door then," he yelled.

"I can't."

"Why not?"

"It's locked."

"I know," Jamie shouted. "Just unlock it!"

"I can't."

"Why not?"

"I can't find the key."

"I'll come in the window then."

There was a big drainpipe by the kitchen door. Jamie started to climb up it.

Half way up, the pipe started to wobble. It was coming away from the wall.

Jamie let go and jumped. He landed with a thud. The bottom half of the pipe had come away from the top half. Water was pouring into the yard.

"There's water coming under the door," Sally yelled.

"Just open the window."

A smashing time

There was a table in the yard that they all sat round in the summer.
Jamie dragged it over to the window.
At that moment there was a crash from the kitchen.

"What's up?" he shouted. "Are you all right?"

"Yes... I... um... I dropped something."

Jamie climbed up on the table and looked into the kitchen.

"There were some things by the sink. I pulled them off," Sally said.

"Is anything broken?"

"Only a bit."

"What?"

"The plates."

"Just the plates?"

"And the cups."

"Everything, then."

"The knives and forks are okay."

"Open the window!"

Sally climbed up by the sink. But she couldn't open the catch.

"Hurry up," Jamie said.

"It won't move. It's stuck. I know what. I'll get a hammer."

"No!" Jamie cried.

Sally came back with a hammer and climbed back up to the window.

"No, don't do that!" Jamie yelled.

"Don't worry. I'll just tap it."

"NO!" Jamie shouted. He could see what would happen.

Jamie jumped off the table. He fell into the pool of water from the broken pipe.

From where he sat he could see Sally tapping the window catch.

"Stop!" he shouted again, but it was too late. There was a crash as Sally missed the catch and hit the glass.

The window smashed.

Jamie's trousers were now so soaked they stuck to him. He climbed back onto the table and very carefully put his hand through the big hole in the window.

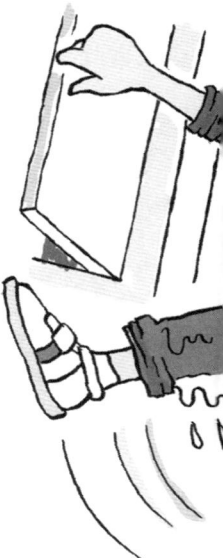

He turned the catch, opened the window and climbed into the dry kitchen.

But Jamie's trainers were so wet that he slipped off the sink. He tried to grab the handle of a cupboard. The cupboard moved but Jamie held on and climbed down safely.

"Look out!" Sally shouted.

The cupboard had moved to an odd angle on the wall, and one door was starting to open.

A real-life ghost

Jamie looked up just as a large bag of flour toppled forward and fell out. To Jamie the bag of flour took a long time to fall. But before he could move, it hit the edge of the sink and exploded.

Flour went everywhere. It looked like a snowstorm.

Jamie was totally covered in flour.

Sally started giggling.

"I suppose you think that's funny," Jamie said.

Sally giggled even more. "You look like a ghost. You're the ghost in the kitchen. Wooooooooo!"

"Very funny… not!" Jamie said.

"Get the mop. And be quick! Mum will be back soon."

First he had to get dry. He pulled off his wet clothes, put them into the tumble drier and turned it on.

There was a noise from the hall.
Mum was back! Jamie grabbed Sally's arm and ran through the hall into the front room.

They were just in time. They heard the front door open and Mum in the hall.

"You two okay?" she called.

"We're fine," Jamie shouted back.

"Did you behave?"

"Of course," Jamie said.

"I'll just put the shopping in the kitchen," Mum said, "then I've got something for you both."

They listened as she walked through the hall and into the kitchen.

At first it was very quiet.
Then Mum screamed.

Mad Mum!

Mum stood in the doorway with a look of horror on her face.

"Well? What happened?"

"There was a ghost in the kitchen," Jamie said.

"You look like you've seen a ghost," Mum said. "You're all white. Did it come through the window?"

"It must have done," Jamie said.

"And did it take your clothes?"

"Um... yes."

"And it put them in the tumble drier, did it?"

"Um… yes… it's very spooky, isn't it?"

"Just tell me this. Why is there a line of white footprints from the kitchen to your feet?"

Mum grabbed Jamie's arm.

"The bathroom! Clean yourself up. Then you can tell me what really went on. And there's no Lucky Bag!"

Sally watched as Jamie went out of the room and up to the bathroom. Then she took down her favourite DVD of cartoons from the shelf.

She put it in the player and sighed.

"Everyone knows there are no such things as ghosts," she said.